Our Prediction

Also by Daniel Tiffany

POETRY

Cry Baby Mystic (Parlor Press, 2021)
The Work-Shy, with Blunt Research Group (Wesleyan Poetry Series, 2016)
Neptune Park (Omnidawn Publishing, 2013)
Privado (Action Books, 2010)
The Dandelion Clock (Tinfish Press, 2010)
Puppet Wardrobe (Parlor Press, 2006)

CHAPBOOKS

The Pig's Valise, with Blunt Research Group (above/ground press, 2024)
Lost Privilege Company, with Blunt Research Group (Noemi Press, 2016)
Brick Radio (Oystercatcher Press, 2014)

THEORY & CRITICISM

My Silver Planet: A Secret History of Poetry and Kitsch (Johns Hopkins University Press, 2014)
In the Poisonous Candy Factory (Capsule Editions, 2013)
Infidel Poetics: Riddles, Nightlife, Substance (University of Chicago Press, 2009)
Toy Medium: Materialism and Modern Lyric (University of California Press, 2000)
Radio Corpse: Imagism and the Cryptaesthetic of Ezra Pound (Harvard University Press, 1995)

Our Prediction

Daniel Tiffany

Fordham University Press   New York   2026

Acknowledgments

Thanks to editors of the following journals where versions of some of these poems first appeared: *Action Spectacle, Fence, Gulf Coast, Three Fold*. And to above/ground press, which published a chapbook of selected poems, *The Pig's Valise* (under the signature of Blunt Research Group) in 2024.

Copyright © 2026 Fordham University Press

All rights reserved. No part of this publication may be reproduced, stored in a retrieval system, or transmitted in any form or by any means—electronic, mechanical, photocopy, recording, or any other—except for brief quotations in printed reviews, without the prior permission of the publisher.

Fordham University Press has no responsibility for the persistence or accuracy of URLs for external or third-party Internet websites referred to in this publication and does not guarantee that any content on such websites is, or will remain, accurate or appropriate.

Fordham University Press also publishes its books in a variety of electronic formats. Some content that appears in print may not be available in electronic books.

Visit us online at www.fordhampress.com.

For EU safety / GPSR concerns: Fordham University Press, Joseph A. Martino Hall, 45 Columbus Avenue, 3rd Floor, New York, NY 10023, fordhampress@fordham.edu

Library of Congress Cataloging-in-Publication Data available online at https://catalog.loc.gov.

Printed in the United States of America

28 27 26   5 4 3 2 1

First edition

Contents

We   1

Once all pillows   3

If to grow less   4

Facing home   6

Why are we not deceived   8

If the world is a mistake   10

Who might as well   11

No we do   12

You can run   13

With all there is   15

To come back to   16

We can think exactly how   17

That's not us   18

Our hatred of antitheses   20

21

They turn not   22

Why have they thought   23

Together with   25

One by one   26

You'll be surprised   27

It crossed our path   28

But it's the other way   30

Pig   32

As long as the extremities   33

We call carelessly   35

If the old abuses   37

Which in a way   39

Nobody knows   40

Had something not been   42

43

Someone has been staring   44

A thread by which it wants   45

This can't be   46

How have we lost   48

It really does   49

Story of the crevice   50

Who spends an hour   51

53

The cat is playing with   54

Drinks on the table   56

We like what we have not prepared   58

Even not there much   59

That they would count   61

Always before afraid of   62

Normally we can't   63

They find they   65

    66

We say this evening   67

Too much of too little   68

Since one can so   70

We have been thought   71

Saved some   73

Our Prediction

[We]

    We try to stay out of it
if we can, incurables and debutantes
        ruled by the ones hugging the ground,
            eaters of trampled pies
    sharp thistle and stinkweed.

        Pull down the crossbar
        cut a hole in the fence,
snuff the ditch it cries
            and cries unaware.
        No feast but would have
            danger against.

We try to leave a few on the stalk
        red or not red
    faces overrun.

        Strange isn't it
            we're not the only ones in this world
                and sometimes we hide from the others
    no one can remember why

but for the low pile of bedclothes
on a mattress against a dark or dirty wall
really just a coarse sheet too small even
to cover the knock-knock twins dozing off
        in the palazzo at 4 a.m.

Not for us,
why not for us

more like broken through
since some of our pals are drifting towards the cut in the floor
and Bodo's pointy head hangs down a little
over the edge into the open air.

[Once all pillows]

Once all pillows were leaves
        and before that

    a pillow of dust.

      That's our interpretation at least.

      The lung inflates itself to a bell
          cheek puckered touching glowing ground
                  the tips melt away
          why is that

          still fit for use
          or sick with over-use.

      "Out of sight, out of mind"
      stuff that doesn't really make sense
    no reason not to say it anyway,
          the smoky dance hall at a standstill
              even the color of the tickets is upsetting.

              We surrender the prize
            the pig's valise.

16 November 1911. The way she calls "slowly" to the musicians for her sisters but also for herself.

          We prep and prod each other tonight because it's
            going to be a big night, squeezed into a corner
      at the onset of a mood not belonging
    to any losers feeling no pain
        —a snail, possibly, crying in the pan.

[*If to grow less*]

    If to grow less could help
       never quite gone

   heads pivoting as one
a clan propped against a wall

  our calculations
   wiping out everything and everyone
      making efforts to bring us to life
    and when they couldn't
to put up with us as we are.

     Fruitcake had a brainstorm

  wondering why *away*
  comes more than asked
  to add *obey* to *stay*.

     Meanwhile twenty-seven had been had
     for which no word is sufficient.

We broke down and threw our drinks after them
         the ones leaving
   wishing now to think to refuse wishes.

    This can be ours at night

  though not warranted by what
    we hear through a neighbor's wall

       the thundering scream of the seraphim's delight.

It's everything we don't already know
                                      also not to refuse trees
        but when will our blunders be done with us
            the no more to be named
                        hot in the mouth,
            here we go again.

[*Facing home*]

        Facing home
                on and off
          snatching a little rest
            before the owner gets back
            we see the other creatures
pigs and goats
      do any of us really think
        we'll be turned back into sailors?

The animal forehead
      draped with coins
    untrue that we know

        no need to know

           NEVER BE THE SAILOR.

  Had something been forgotten
            an adjustment a turn
      a final step?

    Wires crackle
        discharged on a word
      wrongly subsisting,
    the beautiful parts of the dance
            signaled from below

  the heaviness of the body
      dragged back into the light when
            we might as well admit
        what blinds us for a moment
      the immortal type
               there may be a few of those too.

Clippity-clop
little body little block
        clippity-clop.

[*Why are we not deceived*]

    Why are we not deceived
  if subdued

  as in the presence of animals
    in stalls when you tell them to do something and
  surprisingly they do it.

Light strewn over faces and adjacent floor.

A phone call knocks it over.

29 December 1911. "We lead our friends into the woods." A lake in the trees only there are no trees.

  You can go if you like

    fall and vanish from view
  you could lie there for weeks
      and no one hear you.

        Shall we start over?

  To have no use in cherishing

      miserable factory

nobody thought we went there
     we have our well-wishers thank you.
      Black tails expunge,

     fifty devils' tails
    scouring chins and cheeks

                    pressed up
                  stacked into
            what so hurts the eyes
                          invisible

                      dear no.

[If the world is a mistake]

If the world is a mistake
it is a mistake for everyone.

    Introduction. Beautiful dark room,

          minus this
          minus that

    slowly won over
        jack lit prow seed
          the future ungreeting us at 18-second intervals
and more than all of it called in off with.

    Give a thought to Cuba
        one thing not to be made anything
    wedded from nocturnal resolve

or why should anxiousness be anxiousness?

    In place of which attached to unbecoming
        should it flare up
    let it go out.

We've probably caused a disaster.

We try to apologize

    heads bowed
might they not still be there working,
        be made to ask our name?

[*Who might as well*]

Who might as well have disappeared
                next to next to and does

    where the voice belongs
      where it sometimes says
  it must have belonged.

2 August 1966. A lesson a prayer a little of each in case of emergency before the soul
                                                            resigns bubbling up

                    in other words we each retain
                  a place in the antedated rose

    according to Aristotle, who knew everything.

        What about the surgical tubing wrapped around the neck
    of the device used to keep things in order?

We can't go into that right now.

But if we were asked to name the outfit
        behind our little mishap
            we would totally ship June and Johnny
                Alice and Gertrude
            John and Yoko.
    Hey we shipped the poker tournament
        on Royal Caribbean
      feeling sad to end it like this
  whose light must it be for a boatman
to appear at our heels?

[*No we do*]

                          No we do not. If it
tips toward the unsubsided

    it must be cut from the same useless
            drifting by of things
                    someone's always eager to explain.

Day breaks behind a locked door.

We have now examined our workbench more closely.

        Talk of rubbed off experience
      because it calls further mutinously

              the acoustics favoring
          the coughing in the boxes
                    over the words of the actor.

We manage to think twice about everything.

                  Might it be
          contained unlikely

        the haggard schoolchildren are sitting behind wooden desks
                                        stamping their feet.

[*You can run*]

You can run.

The end is near at least fairly near.

        It must be a common sight
    but mixed with something else

the outbreaks of legerdemain
      cutthroat feelings
           pegged to the golden ration, or is it ratio,
     whose lower end will be found two days later
              swinging in emptiness somewhere.

       One long dream of chairs
    figment dawn dispeller
         there you are

the nest empty though not so
       our replacements always appear
       among the listeners

          we consult with them in the garden
          as to how we might eliminate them.

Meals are brought in from heaven!

     Or how to refuse all the attention we're getting
        what's that
           hammer whirring overhead?

We'll come back to that later.

No flight shadow no measuring table.

We can do what we please
or we can do whatever we please.

[With all there is]

With all there is room for
    in thinking to oneself "not so fast"
        these jawns aren't cheap,
      tangled, stalky, not here

              head between knees
              hands holding shins.

                  You'll never see home.

    Floor like bleached dirt, aha,
      even without
        arrows light up

  and what's never finished
      disowning its familiars,
incomplete roses. Or not aligned

  other souls are being
  licked into shape

do you mind
went one

  grubby see-through any length
  threads are tenderly heads
      blacked out fallen open.

In fact many words are dissolved by the voice already occupied
                            by something else.

[*To come back to*]

To come back to a preparation

>locked lab animals know
who gets the extra pellet
and the weird things you need to do.

>>Once they were all here
that's the idea at least.

>We could almost imagine their spines
turning to smoke halfway
through the exchange
they can cease moderation.

>Sunk animals know
blue scattering away

>>a vast night including everything

>forever personal
and untransmittable.

>"Sailed off into a crack in the lake" is the phrase
you often heard a century ago.

Somebody drinking out of an imperfect glass guessed their names. Not where it could be left to have them do just what they like they say.

>Bare walls when the light comes on.

>>Not only gleaning but if they lie down
watching it not be allowed to happen.

[*We can think exactly how*]

We can think exactly how we found out
what keeps happening to us.

    Like when someone shouts "there it is"
    aren't they also probably muttering "it's
            not there" under their breath
            neatly touching off
            the day after tomorrow's botanical surprise?

But once you've crossed the threshold
you must hold your tongue

        because certain relationships may be felt
        distinctly even if they can't be perceived.

It's not so easy to explain
you must simply accept it as a fact.

          And none of this milky
          tideways jabber ever gets
       where it's going

        nor does it help us
      survive the first day
          the standing at
                the paltry furnace and the getting out.

        A worthless individual
            strange as it may seem
    the kind we're always hunting around
      for usually lives next door.

[*That's not us*]

                That's not us there
            hands tied behind our backs
apparitions keepers what day is this
                eating through the phonolapsis
        of the cutinary lining at the foot of noon
                        mouth roped off
                                and the appalling Cornelius de Pauw.

              What's your plan?

Grab the wheel of the car trying to run you down
                        and drive it yourself
              staying on target
                      the axis of the clavicle if that can be said
                                          or done.

        But let's be careful not to misread this moment.

We are on the hunt for constructions. We come into a room and find
              them heaped in a corner tabulating
"number-words" month/date/year to arrive at the "K factor"
(K stands for *Konstruction*), the cross sum of a calendar date:
            January 1, 1974 yields a K factor of 13 = 1+1+7+4.
      Numbers are not mathematics in Hanne Darboven's writing practice.
Who wouldn't like to be a constellation in the sky?

              Only writing is helpless.
              It cannot live in itself,

> never mind the door, the daily count of "in-house letters"
>   is why we are spared,
>   skipping the beauty contest
>   if we could just
>   get out of here.

[*Our hatred of antitheses*]

Our hatred of antitheses is complete.

    How they curl up and cannot
be straightened mere clues
      swelling in the hands

        unexpected but not surprising
and they have always been around

          always the same medium size
starting with the prospect of infinity

          a shoe-tree
        subject to incomprehensible power.

23 September 1917. She seemed to want to help. Flashback to forecast of default which could not be known, capped, discarded, going somewhere to be harnessed.

        You wouldn't be wrong to think this is happening all over again.

    And the vehicle as though out of control begins sliding
                backwards pulling us after it
        all thoughts of completion
          carried off by a lullaby of sorts
        the nocturnal emptiness of the bridge
           exposed suddenly when the clattering stops.

      It's just the way it sounds
        once upon a time
         10% contained
    what is exile oh yes what is exile
we'll just try to say everything not something.

Are the woods still there?

    The woods are still almost there.

[*They turn not*]

They turn not their backs to the scenery.

    But liking strife awhile
  could they put a private anagram
        right up in there there
      like the close-talker on one of those old crime shows?

  Go sit in the truck

wear some rib-eye,
    fringy-average power
flicked up after instead
    of being attached to the alternatives.

    Houred at from behind
  the word "once" ruffles
the unlifting darkness hindered by
      memory would you call it
  a conversation if nobody
else is talking?

    Truly we can't remember a single face.
        We knew them.

Make them be after not at least ready
should they be settled strangely

      a bit of singing on the floor below
the occasional door slamming in the hallway.

[*Why have they thought*]

Why have they thought
we sold what we bought?

    A door is not bought twice.

        Inching lifelong habit
           to a corner here shadowless
     same off
        try again.

What is the question?

                They might be thought
to be well caught but are we not permitted
            to ask how they like it

      each one not entirely sound
            or settled by its replacing.

All understood only just almost never always the same.

We know that.

And they know that.

Of course they do. Rivers could
   be sick men going into convulsions
         in the moonlight and why are theirs
   filled with what is until they reach ours?

    Heads back front
  as on a trestle or do we mean axle,
     when we're not better
      we are here,
for the new protocol everyone is worried about introduces itself
by retreating into a maze of hypotheticals and sort of loses its way,
    dragging its feathered limb at odd angles through the phased-out unrest,
        this goneness, this Eden turned hex backwards.

[*Together with*]

Together with a clothes rack pushed into the middle of the room
    and all the far-away influences

        who cannot please conceal
        nor need they find need they a wish
            (something obtained without
                first getting a good look at it).

    Our colleagues speak out of turn.

            If they were faithful or as bought
                or could be checked

    and pleading they would call it all they know

  nor might they be more enclosed
    their faces soon covered with a weird gray material
with clever slits for the eyes and mouth
  and probably the nose
      would they be presently be spared?

[One by one]

One by one we woke up worrying if we'd laid the culprit in the wrong hole.

Here's how it works, though—
being real means not being inside a single one of us.

    Then there are those who say to themselves
                "keep your eye on that bunch"
        without finding it necessary
           to strap anyone into the chair and stop
                the doll's heart with a penny.

So few people are we.

So few people are me.

    Come hither neither
        blackballed
        galloping through

demanding in return
    we oblige them to go anywhere.

        Remember how we could not be permitted
to disturb them
    had they so much as asked?

           Despised and unrefuted
           that kind of thing.

           A speck of dirt.

We're not going to try to describe what we see walking around.

[*You'll be surprised*]

        You'll be surprised if you call us

    how we show up like cops and wreck the place
                            and put you away,
         one heart one desire
       except the eyes
     talked into canceling whatever
we process at 20,000 leagues.

We might be deceived
ten finger shadow

    spotted with breath

       whereas if we say
   there's a way out somewhere

      a signal beckons from the cliffs—
what's to become
   of the wish to know it's gone. It's gone.

        We could be cut down at noon
     why not obey
         whether or not we hear the command?

Firewood burns
precisely because it burns!

     We vow not to think about things
          as being present.

[*It crossed our path*]

It crossed our path coming up from below.

    No one had ever seen anything like it
        though we do seem to recall hearing
a branch rustling feebly overhead.

  It wandered off everywhere
      like language only later
          developing a habit
          and all the trapdoors
             because it works differently with them to come out of them.

            Trying to block
     the sound of harm being done
      behind the walls of our room
           without knowing where to go
      unable to stop
          never saying a word.

    Whatever it demands
    mind what you say

           now's not the time for to have it fasten
    more than which we can redeem.

Pelts with buds at.

  We call it reveling.

So much for that description,
a river, the forest couldn't be there.

It's best to issue frequent warnings we're told.

Our distaste for close observation is unwavering.

[*But it's the other way*]

                But it's the other way around
        say when with spitting sorry to say
            it tears all wherewith
          what can be not now.

Someone fetched you back
and here we are!

We can have no illusions
or be prepared not to be baffled.

What could possibly make us want to listen to you?

        Even if you change your story the spike would still
be there protruding from his shattered forehead
                having resembled it
                        our last decade

              veiling those
              who went before

            eyes alone unover given

                    must not do go
                  like blades of grass.

The art of combining is not our fault.

            And don't forget Kropotkin!

        Smiled at by him
            we had a slight spell of faintness
                    stifling the earth
            we got over it and
      remembered it a few minutes later

as something long forgotten.

[*Pig*]

        Pig on a spit

   strange expression
it doesn't sound right somehow.

            If only things didn't happen
   to us forever.

        Hours stand still they say
             rumors fuzzball
          reconnaissance

fizzy tab down her shorts
must be something
    to it though

       something once we
    feel it charmed life
          readily not here
to complain and they ask us
        what the heck are we doing?
       We don't know.

   What is it that doesn't matter
to anyone? We don't know.

     We don't matter to anyone.

   And they make us watch these youtubes
What's the Best Kept Secret of Successful People,
          the five secret habits, the real secret.

[*As long as the extremities*]

As long as the extremities are perfectly stable
                        it's hard for us to judge.

      Best not to think of certain things

         since we own them
         and disconnect and know them so well inside them

                 in order to obtain that bombshell perfection.

      We notice a tiny crowd at the entrance
    and vistas though not having to drink

first from face through hole
        then back through face

    with their welcome
    or not at all

        then topple left

               clothes brushing up against
     the thing over there's
  more there.

Oh Dior
  bees walls
    tell ray
      unworn

no dancing the phrase "last day
of the month" incomprehensible,

        downcast words making us believe
        we're still here. Yesterday, wasn't it?

[*We call carelessly*]

        We call carelessly the door to open

   which if they refuse to unlatch
   no one can rush to close.

Let them be ours therefore disabling.

Has anyone mentioned the idea of the mass ornament
       aka the Baader-Meinhof effect
             having something to do
     with "the insurmountable" at the time
                    with getting from *a* to *b*

         or with the lash not counting what goes in?

19 February 1972. Incautious to admit fear calls the deputies out of the woods
as if someone had lit a lamp to help them find their way.

                        Foams out with for not so keen
       bystander shifts neck from side to side again
                and like some kind of invalid.

   Secretly officials
  meet and could with any stay of regulation
manage which they may have in any case a hearing.

Or if they permit ours in a glass
better not be strange in walking.

        Oh yes not yet
         discoveries
     force themselves on people

                    a fur-trimmed silk blouse for example
                    bare throat close-fitting gray hat
      or the "balloon-carried light" explanation we're still trying
                to understand the brute leaving his village behind
                                                without a word of farewell.

[*If the old abuses*]

If the old abuses go unattended
    all sensation from the neck down signs off,

        trotting animal
        the word clicks shut
            over backwards no sound

        in the scares, become
        snail-like comparatively.

And the shortage of time is it not
    what trances bemuse a spittle

        shared off amongst,
    pecked up.

        We don't know what to be on our own.

        Divide division from the horse
    close sheer white all gone
    features crack and little holes.

  It was we could not say
 the usual stuff
    having been long ago not knowing what to feel

    the clarity of events
        barely subsisting
on the ruins of the whole anecdote.

We could often be caught liking it,
              oh we could,

      her mouth open like a twinkling eye.

[*Which in a way*]

Which in a way is not even a question
since we fell asleep in the underbrush.

    A noise awakened us
        everything feeling itself
  to be a thought
          even the vaguest of feelings

when time would have done its work.
It's not now we could answer.

    Special methods of thinking
         every piece of the story runs
around homeless and drives us
           away from it.

        Hedge feint bluff
      not that it matters
         we're still thinking we could
    slip in under the eyelids
           —parted, need not be parted—
      a bluish gleam peeps through!

[*Nobody knows*]

Nobody knows
  we here

                soul's memory
                black box

        invisible shirts

              break-in
              tweekers set up shop

      night like or night like do
    sad gist to peed yeah

  mole suite
  mole people.

Start with the antlers
peel back shit
      tick for into in
        no time to be eight
    and late cracking
           doorskins out-
        lets blinds.

    Toothbrush it.

        Were that sway ten cold
        spewed on by

we ever hear you
talk that way again

                 must be tipping
           benjis somewhere

    nonstop home.

[Had something not been]

Had something not been overlooked

nuisance breach hearsay

   no contest
        all presumedly now we shirk
        to be in their shuddering.

We have even stopped begging.

  No candle no matches no need
       but why the hustle beside the undoing

              if they are almost through with us is it
              not as we submit a blessing
              to have forgotten as many times

          not counting the 700 paintings
          hidden in the walls of a derelict house
       on the outskirts of Prague.

A gaff and by that we mean a large hook
     dredging up a pair of glasses
   a shoe a belt

      now even not the name
      could they be exactly alike
      the whirl of particles
           and the stick attached to it.

19 July 1910. Slept, awoke, slept, awoke, miserable life. Helpless half knowledge of when and where. Hatred of active introspection.

[*Someone has been staring*]

Someone has been staring at those flawless fingertips for quite a while.

    It's not always the one you think
who goes through with it.

        Stanzas are done

              vacancy is tempting
      or rather mainly used
     by finger-thoughts
about—
      about what?

        In front of it once
    is the partition
             thrown out upwards

between throat and chin
      would seem to be the most rewarding place
to stab but rewarding perhaps only in one's
                imagining of the deed.

        You expect to see—what—
the unstoppable gush of blood,
    sinews, tiny bones.

            And if it's one of us
    who would know or care?

[*A thread by which it wants*]

    A thread by which it wants
  to be lowered down below
where it sees itself gleam

      absence better than not before
              gown chore lug tar
        one at a time

        or certain beehive tombs
        if that can be said.

The gaps in the story should have convinced us
we really were hearing that scraping sound
    not how could "never" be misunderstood
        but the same restless terrified look
            guarded by words

        as if we don't know
      what we're actually doing here.

        And again the squalor
        the better part of

the wreckage cannot be ours
    bells drifting back and forth
        with the tide. *Wrong.*

     A small lever somewhere secretly released
          none of us awake yet
and suddenly the whole apparatus lunges forward.

[*This can't be*]

                                  This can't be life,
            ants go marching through your heart
     signaling the cut-off, and the only way around it
                      can get your name on a list.

In the abstract that's how things work
                seized by the collar dragged through
        the streets pushed through the door.

                Cakes bake cakes
            and that makes cake and cakes polite.

          A new perlustration of Cahokia. For instance

     mouth white, seam
  sewn, invisible

     like heels sewn
     together, right angle, invisible.

    We do not wish to say what we think.

           Same remark for the shoemakers
                    a militant faction.

We see flowers at our feet
and it's the others we see

   not knowing where to go

            because no use could be found
for any of them but our father
            fortunately he died
            when we were young.

                  He stopped moving
            and tried to pass himself off
                        as himself
                  waiting for us to get into position.

[*How have we lost*]

How have we lost the thread
of how we came to be alike
      bolting and passing away
      and scarce could run

            startled at the sight
                of the two amidst the hay
                so odd and so grotesque
              what the thing could be

            bolting and passing away
            and scarce could run

the fields after hay
    plowed on the hay
    not on the day

        the pasture strangely turned
           by what we must have seen
         a hundred times before
    come for me come for you

        come for me and you.

[*It really does*]

It really does feel like someone is asking us
                to stay here and stay away.

                    All this cannot be mixed up.

    We bend slowly backwards
        knees hung above
             the swinging of arms
        head best gone.

                Anything wrong with that?

    Lids flicker
        body fixed *ding*
fixed elsewhere
            the seethe of lid.

    That is how we remember however.
        It can be just as well known
    correspondingly despite
a delay of delayed

    often very changed to churn.

            Crowned out
            bunched over

        by so many given
            lone unover given.

Bare white legs white floor.

        And we used to wake feeling nothing at all.

[*Story of the crevice*]

Story of the crevice in the glacier

        speaking without for on
                the prowl somewhere
    we can make conjectures too.

  Run your little finger along your eyebrow
                  for instance.

        Little block heart
        stippled not more than once at all.

  Nowhere does anyone
      ask after you.

  But how can there be this difference
between once in a while and very often and not at all,

                near the house, near a Willow,
        near *this* Willow for the thousandth time.

[*Who spends an hour*]

    Who spends an hour on the sofa not thinking
        once about jumping-out-the-window?

                No tide is perplexed.

            Funny isn't it
                how hands sometimes smell of the woods
                and hair smells of tobacco
        and leaves smell of tea and flowers.

      There's nothing to be done.

A guy keeps picking up a cigarette over and
over again without realizing it.

          You can make it at most or most at it
              there's nobody inside us.

30 August 1912. When we say we never got out of bed today we mean someone in
the hall quickly turned a key in our door and for a moment there were locks all over

                skin and bones

    as if we were the ones searching for a way out of the hallway
and at short intervals
  a lock was opened or shut
        one after another

    just as much as they could as they fasten
                crying through the lock.

There should not be this use in uselessness.

        We are not absent
for any other purpose
            it can't be far

        we'd have to hunt around for a whole year
                to find one true feeling in ourselves.

We could go on with this.

[*The cat is playing with*]

The cat is playing with the goats.

Or would it be a nuisance to feel affection
               for nobody
                      no one at all
             for lack of a better word
       reality was soon restored.

            One solution would be to admit
we are merely each other's mistake
                 momentarily ill
      which explains why these lines may
        sound familiar to you.

         And if it's well known it is well known
     what may be carried
       under the arm like a bundle
         traces blurs signs
     all wedged together
we can feel its
       fluttering twisted length.

               Don't try to explain
           just drop quietly into the river.

          Dropping probably seems so attractive
        because it reminds us of being pushed

              to please the one given
           special right to be a listener

but even the listener is questioned
           uselessly of course
      so many things to hide

                and if someone is riding hurt
      could we be taught to be allowed?

[*Drinks on the table*]

Drinks on the table scarcely touched

        nor was the place as we remembered it
save the little boards screwed against the temples
                a segment cut from the back of the head
           and the sun peering down into it.

    How many hours to go?

        Don't worry she says.

              Whereas a bird
        threading the endlessness will make it
        alright—think about that later—
never throw anything away,
        sleeping raw materials, frenched headlights,
            ugh hole ticked for into with.
                Some say inconceivable now.

        Are we broken?

Aye, how can it not be alone not
liked never but this changelessness?

        We are to begin again yesterday.

Everyone knows about the step ladder
on the slope leading down to the water.

It's always in the same place
but you can only see it in the Fall
             and Winter too

        lying there in the dark grass.

[*We like what we have not prepared*]

We like what we have not prepared before until now.

      From then on naturally
      we summon people to us
      a crook of the finger is enough

a quick unhesitating glance.
They clothe us and give us money.

      We accept their invitation without delay.
      Hooray for the bathroom! Girls in the woods
                  or a thousand mirrors,
                  the old fate steals over us

      but the horror is mostly schematic.

One would prefer to close one's eyes
as one sometimes does

running through the park swinging branches
only to come back to wondering
      what is truly ours,
  a miserable substitute for everything.

To be close to the fire.

And a film about the history of separatist movements
                      if there's time.

[*Even not there much*]

Even not there much as it is
       in the latest rejection

             it sent some gold across the water.

                 The general effect is the same
    in keeping with sentences elevated in the middle
        by one or two jolts
            opening the mouth to its full upright
         and locked position.

We used to not be able to forget
how they always say thank you

        before we can finish our little speech.

Or this variant: someone calls to us
and before we can even draw breath

        we have been dismissed.

      Strange days not seen through yet.

          Phase official poke
          came meek how's

not exactly immune.

            SOS
        bit-open bud

spluttering path.

Are we indifferent?
Not exactly.

The bathroom is ours.

[*That they would count*]

        That they would count or kneel
for which they had been frightened not to do

              and what next
                  which either fetched into horseplay
                      cloaked in a mirror.

We see it's not that but something else
              keeping yes and no unsplit,
        free command of the world
      at the expense of its laws.

  There is no yellow
      here but by design
after all what is a garden
          only a voice borrowing itself from the seedbed,
            small gaping sound.

              If you live with a secret
          come home
all who have been shut in their sense
all should boisterous make it
not if at once to do.

This can be made a reason why.

            We see the poison flower
            but no birds
            getting in our way

      no birds bugging us,
everything theater.

[*Always before afraid of*]

        Always before afraid of unending
              could that be what happened
having forgotten how things work

        nobody could give us a reason.

            Too late
        it splits wide open
thready swollen patched invisibly
      how much harder it is
            to keep shoveling
      to make out the faces

        when they're right under your feet.

6 June 1922. Nobody held back. We once made a kind of discovery in the woods.

      No "and yet" substitutions please
         dime hat dub each
according to the devil's expression

        unwinding "sexual etiquette"
    because the world loans us
a hint of calamity upstream
      swept through a broken fence
            for all to see it's a nymph

      a dead woman's child
      glimpsed through the fog.

We wonder why they even mention what they like.

[*Normally we can't*]

Normally we can't see
   even what's right in front of us
         nor do we hear much,
   we don't pay attention.

       It can't be much longer now.

     Human kindness is not really on our bucket list.

 Or so we thought.

     Anyone know of a blown-out shed
    where the bean-plant climbs?

        No way in, none out,
            leave it at that—
     at for under the midst of us,
      wandering empty hospitable midst.

Evening approaching. Same five words. Aha.

          They hand out that prize
       when it's no longer ours.

   Cheek nestled up
      against a missing person
  found with a stump of a hand.

      Still, we'd prefer to know
    what they make us of,
     we hear the door slam

the eye breaks away from the flowers

        nor which they try not to dream up
                the passing hour
          its inmost reserves
  thrown onto the street.

[They find they]

They find they can always retouch
                to make this seem theirs,

        no point in apologizing again.

2 October 1911. Sometime during the night it cut us all to pieces unhindered.

        Our house must be
             struck from the list of places to visit.

  They tell us to sit on the bed and wait

uninvited
    clothes dripping
    not wet but dripping

           always the same thing
      proposing itself to our dismay

          uninvited guests
  holes mouth white seam

              invisible all known without.

There we've answered we've answered something.

Never come back here whatever you do.

[*We say this evening*]

We say this evening as if it were always the same evening
                                   but aren't there two evenings?

    We decide not to name them
             much as it is allowed
  not their names but ours

       an autobiography in two instances

                           a foil of near
                                  stony ground
               can sharply not be known

  unreprieved if what's
       trimmed down by the head
               falls out with.

9 October 1911. We are convinced that we (and we alone) deceive the world.

To be so lost and not have the sense to regret it.

                   Get started on the woodpile with the maul.

       Single block, arms fast to sides, no hold.

[*Too much of too little*]

                Too much of too little
      had some chance remark by almost anyone
                  flung our regrets into the "third zone" of icy bodies
        which could explain why it's pointless really to try
to avoid weird situations.

     Even what has been withheld
as fast as not so fast
          a flicker of half-lies.

    It's only the beginning of course
         always only the beginning

            the guy in the next room is hammering a nail into the wall.
                We see through it down to the bed
                      that too is ours

      and somewhere help is waiting.
      The beaters are driving us closer.

So much for that explanation.

    Back to your question.

          It's not like we just sit around all day
        deserting ourselves
              waiting to be hauled away.

The tenants had gone back into their rooms

>   to resume their senseless tasks
> though we did them no harm
>   —to everyone's surprise.

>   It's none of our business.

[*Since one can so*]

    Since one can so easily
misread the signals

    or confuse a cloud for a giant cartoon
               hinting at the formula the trick
       of looking away burns into
             our surroundings

         so as to keep us
from losing it altogether.

What's this new trouble
     don't you see

     it's always the same night
it too has its evenings its mornings
             and evenings,

    a pause in mistaken,
       a moon grows in the reeds
where the frost takes the mouse

the impassable true
    ancestral shape
  nearby like anything lost.

[We have been thought]

We have been thought not to respect ourselves.
To have been sold as wishes

what's the worst that could happen
               change *bare* to *ne'er*
                 contraction of never
                     though it will huddle one day
   by itself *queer cove ache a*
                     shun ask.

               Got your eye on heaven
               better stop this stuff.

      Sore gain of a world
      if we next from then on
      have it as not diminished
      and not nearly there.

               Don't stop for any reason.

Not that we know what we want
and we don't want to know what we want.

21 July 1913. To be pulled in through the ground-floor window of a building by a rope tied around your neck and yanked up through all the ceilings, walls, furnishings, attics.

Not even ours is ours

the house already locked up
eyes fixed elsewhere

arms trunk head
all trebled off and wedged in half

as before at position *a*
that much memory almost never.

[Saved some]

Saved some face no reason
caught red-handed once or twice

we couldn't manage without stalling
to prepare for liking and liking it.

        That's the mistake we made one of them
                we tore up the secret recipe
           a shortcut to the old swamp-
joy of being knocked to the ground again.

                It's unavoidable
         we start walking up and down
            one side of the room

from a walk we break into a trot
and from a trot into a gallop.

          Really, do we have to explain
      what keeps following us around

no one knows where it came from
        and it's not all that great
        the same night suffered up into which
           there and not-there
              we promise to forget them all
       had they as much as disappeared

   might they not be there waiting
        heart breath no sound
   hold a mirror to the lips.

Daniel Tiffany is the author of collections of poetry from presses including Wesleyan, Action Books, Noemi, Tinfish, Parlor Press, and Omnidawn, His poems have been published in many journals, including *Poetry, Boston Review, Brooklyn Rail, Lana Turner, Bomb,* and *Paris Review.* In addition to his own writing, he has published translations of texts from French, Greek, and Italian. Tiffany is also the author of five volumes of academic criticism from presses including Harvard, Chicago, and Johns Hopkins. His entry on "Lyric Poetry and Poetics" can be found in the current edition of the *Oxford Encyclopedia of Literature,* and he is a recipient of the Berlin Prize from the American Academy in Berlin. www.danieltiffany.com

www.ingramcontent.com/pod-product-compliance
Lightning Source LLC
Chambersburg PA
CBHW060503080526
44584CB00015B/1531